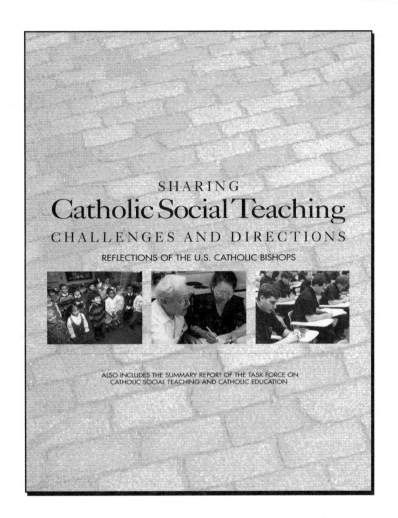

SHARING
Catholic Social Teaching
CHALLENGES AND DIRECTIONS
REFLECTIONS OF THE U.S. CATHOLIC BISHOPS

ALSO INCLUDES THE SUMMARY REPORT OF THE TASK FORCE ON
CATHOLIC SOCIAL TEACHING AND CATHOLIC EDUCATION

Leader's Guide to
Sharing
Catholic Social Teaching

UNITED STATES CONFERENCE OF CATHOLIC BISHOPS • WASHINGTON, D.C.

The *Leader's Guide to "Sharing Catholic Social Teaching"* was coordinated by the Department of Social Development and World Peace and the Department of Education as part of their plans and priorities for 1999. It is intended to be used as a resource in conjunction with the bishops' statement *Sharing Catholic Social Teaching*. This material has been reviewed by His Eminence Roger Cardinal Mahony, chairman, Domestic Policy Committee; the Most Reverend Theodore M. McCarrick, chairman, International Policy Committee; and the Most Reverend Francis B. Schulte, chairman, Committee on Education. The *Leader's Guide* is authorized for publication by the undersigned.

Monsignor Dennis M. Schnurr
General Secretary
NCCB/USCC

In 2001 the National Conference of Catholic Bishops and United States Catholic Conference became the United States Conference of Catholic Bishops.

Illustrations: Ade Bethune, page 8; CNS, pages 28, 33, 34, 39.

Scripture texts used in this work are taken from the *New American Bible*, copyright © 1991, 1986, and 1970 by the Confraternity of Christian Doctrine, Washington, DC 20017 and are used by permission of the copyright owner. All rights reserved.

Excerpts from *Vatican Council II: The Conciliar and Post Conciliar Documents* edited by Austin Flannery, OP, copyright © 1975, Costello Publishing Company, Inc., Northport, N.Y. are used with permission of the publisher, all rights reserved. No part of these excerpts may be reproduced, stored in a retrieval system, or transmitted in any form or by any means—electronic, mechanical, photocopying, recording, or otherwise—without express written permission of Costello Publishing Company.

First Printing, January 2000
Second Printing, June 2002

ISBN 1-57455-366-6

Leader's Guide to
"Sharing Catholic Social Teaching"

Contents

Preface

The *Leader's Guide to "Sharing Catholic Social Teaching"* was prepared in response to a recommendation of the Subgroup on Religious Education, Youth Ministry, and Adult Education of the Task Force on Catholic Social Teaching and Catholic Education. In the summary report of the task force, issued January 5, 1998, and included in *Sharing Catholic Social Teaching*, recommendation three of the subgroup read, "Promote ongoing integration of Catholic social teaching inclusive of liturgical catechesis in catechetical/educational programs by developing a basic formation component in programs for adults engaged in ministry" (p. 15).

ABOUT THE AUTHOR

This guide was written by Dr. Stephen M. Colecchi, who is currently the special assistant to the bishop as well as the director of the Office of Justice and Peace of the Catholic Diocese of Richmond. He worked for many years in the field of religious education as a parish director of religious education and as a Catholic high school religion teacher.

ACKNOWLEDGMENTS

The subgroup acknowledges the support and sponsorship of this publication by William H. Sadlier, Inc., Loyola Press, and the United States Catholic Conference. Susan Morris of the Diocese of Springfield, Ill., wrote the "Prayer for Peace and Justice." William M. Ippolito, executive projects director at William H. Sadlier, Inc., provided valuable support to the work of the subgroup.

SUBGROUP ON RELIGIOUS EDUCATION, YOUTH MINISTRY, AND ADULT EDUCATION

Dr. Gerard F. Baumbach
Subgroup Chair
Executive Vice President and Publisher
William H. Sadlier, Inc.

Dr. Thomas Bright
Center for Ministry Development
Naugatuck, Conn.

Dr. Barbara Campbell
Director of Catechetical Services
Loyola Press

Mr. Rich Fowler
Director of Diocesan Relations
Department of Social Development and World Peace
United States Catholic Conference

Reverend Raymond B. Kemp
Senior Fellow, Woodstock Theological Center
Georgetown University

Elaine McCarron, SCN
Regional Director for Religious Education
Diocese of Wilmington, Del.

Mr. Daniel Mulhall
Assistant Secretary for Catechesis and Inculturation
Department of Education
United States Catholic Conference

Mr. Stephen Palmer
Associate Executive Director
Department of Religious Education
National Catholic Educational Association

Mr. Neil Parent
Executive Director
National Conference of Catechetical Leadership

Maureen Shaughnessy, SC
Assistant Secretary for Catechesis and
    Leadership Development
Department of Education
United States Catholic Conference

Introduction

Catholic social teaching is a precious treasure—unfortunately, one that is too often buried (cf. Mt 13:44), a shining light too often kept "under a bushel basket" (Mt 5:15). In a world threatened by attacks on human life, human dignity, and creation itself, the Church's social justice teaching offers hope. In a world that has enormous human and technological resources at its disposal for human development, Catholic social teaching offers to humanity a direction and a social vision that mirrors the values of the reign of God that Jesus announced and embodied.

In the 1998 statement *Sharing Catholic Social Teaching: Challenges and Directions* (Washington, D.C.: United States Catholic Conference), the bishops of the United States declared, "The sharing of our social tradition is a defining measure of Catholic education and formation" (p. 3). They recognized the "commitment and creativity of so many educators and catechists" in sharing Catholic social teaching and acknowledged, "Sadly, our social doctrine is not shared or

> **Catholic social teaching offers a direction and social vision that mirrors the values of the reign of God.**

taught in a consistent and comprehensive way. . ." (p. 3).

There is no lack of goodwill among catechetical and educational leaders; they want to share the social teaching of the Church, but they often are not sure of the concrete content of the teaching or lack the confidence to integrate it into formational activities in appropriate ways. This is especially true of the aspects of the Church's social justice teaching that prophetically challenge today's culture. Formational leaders sometimes shy away from presenting the Church's teaching on controversial but crucial social issues because they are not sure they can confidently present the Church's teaching and avoid unproductive ideological debates.

The *Leader's Guide to "Sharing Catholic Social Teaching"* was prepared in response to a recommendation of the Subgroup on Religious Education, Youth Ministry, and Adult Education of the Task Force on Catholic Social Teaching and Catholic Education. In the summary report of the task force, issued January 5, 1998, recommendation three of the subgroup reads, "Promote ongoing integration of Catholic social teaching inclusive of liturgical catechesis in catechetical/educational programs by developing a basic formation component in programs for adults engaged in ministry" (p. 15). The *Leader's Guide* is written specifically to equip church leaders and educational trainers.

The overall goals of this guide are as follows:

1. To familiarize formational leaders with Catholic social teaching
2. To help leaders integrate Catholic social teaching into their formational activities
3. To enable leaders to engage children, youth, and adults to act on the teaching in both charitable service and action for justice

This *Leader's Guide* is designed for diocesan leaders of educational and catechetical ministries, catechists and parish directors of religious education, Catholic school principals and teachers, Rite of Christian Initiation of Adults leaders and teams, youth and young adult ministry leaders, and those engaged in sacramental preparation and a range of other activities that form people in faith. The guide is designed to help formational leaders to infuse Catholic social teaching consistently into their teaching, programs, and activities.

A flexible resource designed for use in a number of different group settings, this *Leader's Guide* can also be used for study and reflection by individuals committed to incorporating Catholic social teaching into programs of faith formation for children, youth, and adults.

To create a society with more just laws and social structures, we need prayerful people of moral integrity.

The guide can stand on its own, but the study of Catholic social teaching will be more complete if used by individuals with an overall familiarity with Catholic moral teaching. Catholic social teaching focuses our moral attention on social structures—cultural values, social institutions, public policies, and economic practices.

This focus requires social analysis and community action—moral actions that promote positive social change. But to create a society with more just laws and social structures, we need prayerful people of moral integrity—people personally committed to God's will for a loving, just, and peaceful world.

Learning Objectives

After completing the three sessions of study, participants will be able to achieve seven specific learning objectives:

1. Explain seven themes of Catholic social teaching
2. Describe the sources of the Church's social teaching
3. Identify several biblical passages related to social justice and peace
4. Distinguish between charity and justice as responses to the Church's social mission
5. Use the ART of Catholic Social Teaching model to enrich formational activities
6. Identify ways to adapt social teaching activities for various ages
7. Find opportunities to link the Church's social teaching to liturgical catechesis

Each session outline identifies the learning objectives specific to that session.

Background

This *Leader's Guide* assumes a basic familiarity with recent documents on Catholic social teaching. Before conducting a meeting on the topic, you should have read the following:

- National Conference of Catholic Bishops, *Sharing Catholic Social Teaching: Challenges and Directions* (Washington, D.C.: United States Catholic Conference, 1998)
- National Conference of Catholic Bishops, *Everyday Christianity: To Hunger and Thirst for Justice* (Washington, D.C.: United States Catholic Conference, 1998)
- Pope John Paul II, *On Social Concern (Sollicitudo Rei Socialis)* (Washington, D.C.: United States Catholic Conference, 1988)

Format

This guide contains three principal sections that cover the content and presentation of Catholic social teaching, along with two sections of supplementary material. Each of the three main sections has two parts. The first part presents a brief overview of the section's material. The second part provides a detailed meeting outline to present that section's topic to a group.

The titles of the three sections are

1. Exploring Catholic Social Teaching
2. The ART of Sharing Catholic Social Teaching
3. Sharing Catholic Social Teaching

The supplementary sections include

- Prayers: These can be used for personal reflection and to open and close a meeting.
- Study Sheets: These provide additional information that can be duplicated and distributed for training sessions.

Avoiding Ideological Conflicts

Before applying Catholic social teaching to specific issues, a word of caution is in order. The Church's social teaching is neither liberal nor conservative. It seeks simply to be faithful to God's call. Formational leaders—and all church leaders in their ministerial roles—should carefully avoid the appearance of being partisan or ideological. The key is to remain firmly anchored in the Church's social teaching, especially in its basic themes or principles. As specific issues are explored, people of goodwill might see complex social issues differently. Each of us should strive to be faithful to the teaching and respectful of others in discussing issues.

The Second Vatican Council taught, "Very often [the] Christian vision will suggest a certain solution in some given situation. Yet it happens rather frequently, and legitimately so, that some of the faithful, with no less sincerity, will see the problem quite differently" (*Pastoral Constitution on the Church in the Modern World* [*Gaudium et Spes*] [GS], no. 43).

The council offered this guidance: "[People] ought to remember that in those cases no one is permitted to identify the authority of the Church exclusively with his own opinion. Let them, then, try to guide each other by sincere dialogue in a spirit of mutual charity and with anxious interest above all in the common good" (GS, no. 43).

The following guidelines will help formational leaders to avoid unproductive ideological debates as groups encounter and act on Catholic social teaching.

1. Stay focused on the Church's social teaching, especially its basic themes and principles, regarding human life, human rights, justice, and peace.
2. Acknowledge that persons of goodwill might legitimately disagree over how to apply this teaching in particular circumstances, especially complex social situations.
3. Use the Church's social teaching as a lens to look at the moral and human dimensions of public issues.
4. Encourage dialogue and respect for the dignity of each participant in the discussion.
5. Do not allow anyone to identify the Church with a particular ideology, partisan group, political party, or candidate.
6. Over the course of time, address a wide range of issues of concern to the Church, especially foundational issues of human life and dignity, to avoid the appearance of being ideological. Do not just focus on a few social issues of special interest to you.

Discussion groups function better when they follow basic ground rules. Review these ground rules with the group and get them to agree to the rules before starting a session.

1. Remember the Church's social teaching.
2. Use "I" statements. (Take responsibility for the opinions you express. Do not speak for "them.")
3. Help all to participate. (Do not dominate.)
4. Challenge ideas, not persons. (Avoid questioning the integrity or motives of others.)
5. Stay on the topic.
6. Do not identify the Church with a partisan group.
7. Be respectful and charitable at all times.

How to Use This Leader's Guide

FOR INDIVIDUAL STUDY

Individuals can simply use this guide as a workbook. You can read and work through the text and study sheets at your own pace. Keeping a journal to record personal reflections on discussion questions is highly recommended. Prayer at the beginning and end of each period of study will deepen the experience and anchor it in the Lord. You can use the prayers on pp. 27-28 for this purpose.

FOR GROUP STUDY

Although the option of individual study may be appropriate given personal circumstances, the topic of Catholic social teaching lends itself to group study in a singular way. As the social teaching of the Church reminds us, we are social beings. Social interaction in a group setting can widen and deepen the learning experience. We can learn from one another.

The next sections of the *Leader's Guide* outline three two-hour sessions for exploring the material. These outlines are simply samples, and the time allocations are approximate. A trainer can easily divide them into six sessions lasting an hour or less each. It is also possible to string them together for a day-long training event (about six hours) by making some minor adjustments. Using these outlines flexibly will enable trainers to better meet the needs of their group.

> ## Social interaction in a group setting can widen and deepen the learning experience.

Session One
Exploring Catholic Social Teaching

Catholic social teaching is a distinct body of church doctrine with its own primary sources and literature. At the same time, it is related to other areas of the Church's teaching on God, revelation, liturgy, sacraments, personal morality, and prayer. This is why the *Catechism of the Catholic Church* weaves Catholic social teaching throughout its text and also includes in-depth sections on the Church's social teaching and specific social issues in its exploration of morality in part three, "Life in Christ." In the words of the *Catechism*, "The Church's social teaching proposes principles for reflection; it provides criteria for judgment; it gives guidelines for action" (no. 2423).

According to the Catholic bishops of the United States, "far too many Catholics are not familiar with the basic content of Catholic social teaching. More fundamentally, many Catholics do not adequately understand that the social teaching of the Church is an essential part of Catholic faith" (*Sharing Catholic Social Teaching: Challenges and Directions* [SCST] [Washington,

D.C.: United States Catholic Conference, 1998], p. 3). This reality is both a challenge and an opportunity for committed educational and catechetical leaders. The *General Directory for Catechesis* (GDC) states, "By means of catechesis, in which due emphasis is given to her social teaching, the Church desires to stir Christian hearts 'to the cause of justice' and to a 'preferential option or love for the poor,' so that her presence may really be light that shines and salt that cures" (no. 17).

The roots of Catholic social teaching are found in the Scriptures, but its branches continue to grow today. The body of social doctrine grew throughout the centuries as the Church encountered new social situations. The same Holy Spirit who inspired the Scriptures is with

> **The roots of Catholic social teaching are found in the Scriptures, but its branches continue to grow today.**

the Church as we "read the signs of the times" in each new culture and age (*Pastoral Constitution on the Church in the Modern World* [*Gaudium et Spes*] [GS], no. 4). In the words of the *Catechism*, "the Church's social teaching comprises a body of doctrine, which is articulated as the Church interprets events in the course of history, with the assistance of the Holy Spirit, in the light of the whole of what has been revealed by Jesus Christ" (no. 2422). The *Catechism* also says, "The development of the doctrine of the Church on economic and social matters attests the permanent value of the Church's teaching at the same time as it attests the true meaning of her Tradition, always living and active" (no. 2421; cf. John Paul II, *On the Hundredth Anniversary of Rerum Novarum* [*Centesimus Annus*], no. 3).

This past century has been a particularly fertile time for the growth of the Church's social justice tradition. The rapid pace of social and technological change called the Church to respond with courage and creativity. Popes, the Second Vatican Council, bishops' conferences, and individual bishops have all contributed to this body of teaching. Many theologians have helped to apply and advance the teaching. Committed clergy, religious, and lay persons have helped shape the social justice tradition through their witness in the world.

LEARNING OBJECTIVES

After completing this unit of study, participants will be able to do the following:

1. Explain seven themes of the Church's social teaching
2. Describe the sources of the Church's social teaching
3. Identify several biblical passages related to social justice and peace

QUESTIONS FOR PERSONAL REFLECTION

1. About what social issues have the pope or the bishops spoken in recent years?
2. On what basis does the Church speak to social, economic, or political questions?

Sharing Catholic Social Teaching

Read *Sharing Catholic Social Teaching: Challenges and Directions*. The Catholic bishops of the United States issued this statement in response to a report by their Task Force on Catholic Social Teaching and Catholic Education. This *Leader's Guide to "Sharing Catholic Social Teaching"* is a result of one of the recommendations of the task force. The "Catholic Social Teaching: Major Themes" section of the bishops' statement (pp. 4-6) offers succinct discussion of the major

> **This past century has been a fertile time for the growth of the Church's social justice tradition.**

themes of Catholic social teaching and provides the foundation for all that you will do in your sessions.

(Study Sheet 1, on pg. 30, also gives summaries of these major themes.)

The first six of these major themes have been identified and developed in a tradition of papal, conciliar, and episcopal documents. In their statement, however, the U.S. bishops have added a seventh major theme: the command to "care for God's creation." This command, which is not new (cf. Gn 2:15), has become increasingly urgent and complex today as we struggle to preserve the ecology of the earth. The emergence of this major theme is an example of Catholic social teaching growing to meet new demands in society. The teaching's foundation is in the Scriptures, but it grows as part of the Church's living tradition under the guidance of the Spirit of God.

Bring Down the Walls Video

Most church historians trace the modern phase of Catholic social teaching to Pope Leo XIII's landmark encyclical, *On the Condition of Workers (Rerum Novarum)* (1891). An encyclical is a teaching letter written by the pope for the universal Church. In *Rerum Novarum*, Pope Leo XIII addressed dramatic new injustices that had arisen with the Industrial Revolution. In particular, he defended the rights of workers.

The video *Bring Down the Walls* was produced by the United States Catholic Conference in 1991 to mark the hundredth anniversary of the modern phase of Catholic social teaching. The video was produced shortly after the fall of Communism and the Berlin Wall. It uses the image of "bringing down walls" to speak of our continuing call to tear down walls of injustice and indifference. After a brief mention of some historical developments and a few contemporary social issues, the video covers six of the seven major themes of Catholic social teaching. ("Care for God's Creation" is not covered in this video, which was produced before the bishops added that theme.) This list of themes may not be exhaustive, but it is foundational. *Bring Down the Walls* concludes with some suggestions for putting the social teaching of the Church into action.

QUESTIONS FOR REFLECTING ON THE VIDEO

1. What social issues were mentioned?
2. How did any of these issues surprise you?
3. What are some local issues to which you can apply the six themes of Catholic social teaching?
4. What were some of the ways the video suggested that Catholics could act on the Church's social mission?

Themes of Catholic Social Teaching

Study Sheet 1, "Major Themes of Catholic Social Teaching," contains the themes outlined in the video and presented in *Sharing Catholic Social Teaching*. This study sheet can provide an important point of reference for the participants during the sessions and can be a handy reference sheet for them later on.

Official Church Documents

Catholic social teaching is found in many official church documents: papal encyclicals, pronouncements of a church council (in this case Vatican II), and statements by national or regional bishops' conferences (e.g., the National Conference of Catholic Bishops). Study Sheet 2, "Quotes from Official Church

As Catholics we look to the entire witness of the Scriptures, which have social justice woven throughout them.

Documents," can help us become familiar with how these statements express Catholic social teaching. To get a better appreciation for the depth and breath of this extensive body of teaching, you should get copies of some of the documents and read them. For those who have not read many church documents, the more recent statements may be easier to understand because they speak to more contemporary social situations.

Scriptural Foundations

Study Sheet 3, "Some Scriptural Foundations of Catholic Social Teaching," provides an opportunity to read and reflect on a few scriptural references for each of the themes that are the foundations of the Church's social teaching. These passages are not offered as "proof texts" for the teaching, for the Catholic tradition does not rely on quoting isolated passages to prove a point. As Catholics we look to the entire witness of the Scriptures, which have social justice woven throughout them. We also look to the Church's living tradition, which "reads the signs of the times" under the inspiration of the Holy Spirit and advances the teaching in each new age (GS, no. 4).

7

Session 1 Exploring Catholic Social Teaching *(2 hours)*

NOTES

PREPARATION—Read this sample outline and the corresponding sections of the *Leader's Guide*. Secure copies of the *Leader's Guide* or make copies of the handouts that you will need for this session for each participant. You may need a Bible for the prayer. Preview the video *Bring Down the Walls*. Set up a registration table with name tags and a sign-in sheet. Decide ahead of time on a simple, quick way to divide the participants into small groups of four to six persons. You might color-code the name tags for this purpose. Position and test the television and video player, and set the video to the start of the tape. Write suggested "ground rules" in large letters on newsprint to use during the second part of the session. Set up the room so that the participants will be comfortable. Arrange for refreshments. Complete your setup ahead of time so that you are free to greet participants as they arrive.

INTRODUCTION—Introduce yourself. Welcome the participants. Use the overview of Catholic social teaching on p. 5 and the learning objectives on p. 2 to introduce the participants to the topic and purposes of these study sessions. Close your brief remarks by asking the participants to reflect on the two "Questions for Personal Reflection" for one minute. (5 minutes)

OPENING PRAYER—Lead the group in the Prayer of Saint Francis. (They will need copies—see the "Prayers" section, p. 27, in the *Leader's Guide*.) An alternative is to have someone proclaim Luke 4:16-21, followed by everyone praying the Lord's Prayer. If you choose the second option, select a reader ahead of time from those who arrive early and give the person a Bible to prepare the reading. (3 minutes)

INTRODUCTIONS—Ask the participants to briefly introduce themselves to the group. Invite them to share their names, their roles as educational/catechetical leaders, and one social issue (without discussion) about which the pope or bishops have spoken. Ask them to try not to repeat an issue identified by another. See how many different issues the group can name. (If the group is large, you might divide them into smaller groups for introductions.) (7 minutes)

INTRODUCE THE VIDEO—Use the brief description in the *Leader's Guide* to introduce the video, *Bring Down the Walls*. Ask the participants to look for the social issues mentioned in the video, six major themes of Catholic social teaching, and suggestions for how Catholics can act on this teaching. (1 minute)

8

LEADER'S GUIDE TO *SHARING CATHOLIC SOCIAL TEACHING*

VIEW THE VIDEO—*Bring Down the Walls* (12 minutes)

DEBRIEFING THE VIDEO—Use the "Questions for Reflecting on the Video" (p. 6) to help participants to recall some of the major points. Pose the questions to the whole group. Ask them to keep their responses brief. This is not a time for discussion; the goal is to unpack the content of the video. Give quieter members of the group an opportunity to contribute. Affirm vocal individuals and then gently redirect your attention to allow other participants to join in. (7 minutes)

EXPLORING THE THEMES OF CATHOLIC SOCIAL TEACHING— Ask the participants to review Study Sheet 1, "Major Themes of Catholic Social Teaching." Use the text in the *Leader's Guide* on "Themes of Catholic Social Teaching" (p. 28) to call their attention to the addition of a seventh theme, "Care of God's Creation." Quickly divide the participants into prearranged small groups of four to six persons each. Assign each group one or two themes. Ask each small group to read the theme(s) and then to come up with a list of today's social issues for which this theme has implications. They should not try to resolve what should be done for each issue—instead, the goal is to identify some of the social implications of the theme. For example, the first theme has implications for the issues of abortion and the death penalty, among others. Ask each small group to be prepared to do the following with the large group:

1. Select someone to read the theme(s) to the large group
2. Reach consensus on three to five of today's social issues for which this theme has implications

Remind them of how much time they will have. (15 minutes)

REPORTS FROM SMALL GROUPS—Invite each small group to give a one-minute report on each theme. Have each group's spokesperson first read the group's theme to the gathering and then briefly name or list three to five social issues related to the theme. (10 minutes)

BREAK—Have refreshments available. Note the location of restrooms. (10 minutes)

AVOIDING IDEOLOGICAL CONFLICTS—Display the suggested "ground rules." Use the material in the *Leader's Guide* on "Avoiding Ideological Conflicts" (pp. 3-4) to explain the importance of viewing issues with the eyes of faith. Ask the participants to adopt the "ground rules." Do they want to add any? Remind those participants who work with older youth and adults that it is important to use similar ground rules with their groups when they discuss social issues. (5 minutes)

QUOTES FROM OFFICIAL CHURCH DOCUMENTS—Ask the participants to look over Study Sheet 2, "Quotes from Official Church Documents." Use the text of the *Leader's Guide* on "Official Church Documents" (p. 7) to describe briefly the sources of these quotes. Encourage them to consider reading some of these documents. (See Study Sheet 10 for descriptions of these documents.) Quickly divide the participants into the same prearranged small groups of four to six persons each. Ask each group to focus on the same themes from the earlier discussion. Ask them to read each quotation and to discuss these questions after each is read:

1. In what ways does this teaching affirm aspects of our society's laws, economic practices, and values?
2. In what ways does this teaching challenge aspects of our society's laws, economic practices, and values?

Ask each small group to be prepared to do the following with the large group:

1. Select someone to read the quotation(s) to the large group
2. Reach consensus on one major way in which each teaching affirms and challenges our society

Remind them of how much time they will have. (25 minutes)

REPORTS FROM SMALL GROUPS—Invite each small group to give a two-minute summary to the large group on each theme. Have each spokesperson read one of the quotations and briefly describe one major way this teaching affirms and one way it challenges our society. (15 minutes)

HOME STUDY—Ask the participants to use Study Sheet 3, "Some Scriptural Foundations of Catholic Social Teaching," at home in preparation for the next session. Suggest that they also consider reading *Sharing Catholic Social Teaching: Challenges and Directions*, especially its summary of "Catholic Social Teaching: Major Themes" (pp. 4-6). Remind them of the time and place of the next meeting. Thank them for their participation. (2 minutes)

CLOSING PRAYER—Lead the group in the "Prayer for Peace and Justice." (They will need copies—see the "Prayers" section, p. 27.) An alternative is to have someone proclaim Isaiah 58, pausing after verses 3a, 5, 7, 9, 12, and 14 for the group to respond, "Let our light break forth like the dawn." If you select the second option, select a reader ahead of time from those who arrive early and give the person a Bible to prepare the reading. (3 minutes)

MEETING CHECKLIST

Number of people expected:_____

X	MATERIAL/ACTION	X	MATERIAL/ACTION
	Leader's Guides		
	study sheets		
	Bring Down the Walls video		
	video playback equipment		
	Sharing Catholic Social Teaching books		
	name tags		
	sign-in sheet		
	newsprint		
	Bible		
	prayer sheets		
	refreshments		

NOTES

The ART of Sharing Catholic Social Teaching

Charity and justice complete one another. As Catholics we are called to both. Charity alone does not change social structures that attack human dignity and oppress people; however, charity does help meet the immediate needs of persons and families. Justice demands that we change oppressive social structures, but we cannot ignore the urgent needs of persons while we pursue social change. Charity calls for individuals to respond; justice requires communal action.

With their focus on individualism, people in the United States tend to emphasize charity over justice. The challenge for educational and formational leaders is to help Catholics appreciate the demands of both charity and justice. Recalling the words of the Second Vatican Council, the *Catechism of the Catholic Church* reinforces the important distinction between charity and justice: "The demands of justice must be satisfied first of all; that which is already due in justice is not to be offered as a gift of charity" (no. 2446).

> **Charity calls for individuals to respond; justice requires communal action.**

The *Catechism* also speaks of both personal and social sin: The "'sin of the world' . . . can also refer to the negative influence exerted on people by communal situations and social structures that are the fruit of men's sins" (no. 408). The *Catechism* goes on to state that "sins give rise to social situations and institutions that are contrary to the divine goodness. 'Structures of sin' are the . . . effect of personal sins. They lead their victims to do evil in their turn. In an analogous sense, they constitute a 'social sin'" (no. 1869).

The reality of social sin, which is imbedded in social structures, institutions, and laws, requires more of us than individual charity: it requires works of justice. Abortion, racism, discrimination, sexism, genocide, ecological devastation, violence, pornography, and excessive economic inequality are all examples of social sin—structures of sin that also demand action for justice. Study Sheet 4, "Charity and Justice," explores these two essential responses to the Church's social teaching. Charity and justice are two sides of the same coin. While each is unique, each also complements the other. The two columns on the study sheet compare charity and justice.

LEARNING OBJECTIVES

After completing this unit of study, participants will be able to do the following:

1. Distinguish between charity and justice as responses to the Church's social mission
2. Use the ART of Catholic Social Teaching model to enrich formational activities

The ART of Catholic Social Teaching Model

The ART of Catholic Social Teaching is a simple model developed by the Office of Justice and Peace of the Diocese of Richmond to help parishes work for social justice. ART can also help catechetical and educational leaders to integrate Catholic social teaching into their programs.

In its simplest form, the acronym ART stands for Act, Reflect, and Transform. The goal of the ART process is to work for social transformation that mirrors the values of God's reign of justice and peace. Each of the three letters in the acronym also has a secondary meaning that helps guide ministers: Attend, Research, and Transcend. The model will explore each of these elements.

ACT

The initial response of most people to issues of human concern is to *act* to meet the immediate need. For example, we feed the hungry, shelter the homeless, resettle refugees, protect victims of domestic violence, and recycle our trash. Through this type of action, we come in contact with each issue. The issue takes on a face; it becomes more real to us.

But this type of action alone also frustrates us. It does address the pain of people, but it does little to address the causes. People continue to come to us hungry, homeless, battered; they still flee to us from war and oppression. The environment still suffers.

Before educators and formational leaders engage people in direct service to act on social needs, we need to be sure we *attend* to two things: (1) the readiness of our students or parishioners to *act* on this particular social issue, and (2) the dignity of those we intend to serve. It is important to prepare people for what they will experience. They also need to know what to look for as they *act* in service in order to maximize the learning experience. It is equally important that they are sensitized to the dignity of those they serve—and that they are open to learning from the experience and especially from those who are unfortunate.

REFLECT

The next step is to ask, "Why?" Why are people hungry, homeless, uprooted, battered, or discriminated against? Why is the environment damaged? Why are these issues concerns of faith? What does our faith have to say about these social issues and their causes?

We begin to ask deeper questions. What factors contribute to this social problem? Who gains from the current situation? Who loses? Who has power? Who doesn't? Which beliefs and values support the status quo? Which challenge it? What do Scripture and Catholic social teaching have to say? The *reflect* phase of the ART process enables us to explore the underlying causes of poverty, violence, homelessness, war, racism, ecological devastation, and other issues.

> ## The goal of the ART process is to work for social transformation that mirrors the values of God's reign of justice and peace.

It is not enough simply to *reflect* on social questions and the Church's social teaching from our limited personal perspectives or preconceived ideas. *Research* deepens our reflection. We need both academic *research* based on the social sciences and practical *research* that comes from listening carefully to those directly affected by the social issue. Finally, we need to *research* what the Church teaches. This is where the rich tradition of papal, conciliar, episcopal, and theological reflection is a real treasure.

13

> # The task for formational and educational leaders is to engage persons in reflection that leads to both charity and justice.

TRANSFORM

The final step is to *transform* the social structures that contribute to suffering and injustice. Social transformation is a different kind of action. Transformation gets at root causes; it does not stop at alleviating symptoms.

We can *transform* our communities and our world through, for example, changing social values, empowering low-income people, advocating for just public policies, buying or boycotting goods based on social values, adopting lifestyle changes, and investing in socially responsible corporations.

The *transform* phase of ART embodies the kind of action envisioned by the World Synod of Bishops in their 1971 statement *Justice in the World*: "Action on behalf of justice and participation in the transformation of the world fully appear to us as a constitutive dimension of the preaching of the Gospel, or, in other words, of the Church's mission for the redemption of the human race and its liberation from every oppressive situation" (National Conference of Catholic Bishops, *Justice in the Marketplace* [Washington, D.C.: United States Catholic Conference, 1985], p. 25).

As we work to *transform* society, formational leaders must be careful to *transcend* these efforts in two senses. First, we must always *transcend* ideological boundaries and base our work for social transformation on Catholic social teaching, not on any ideology. Second, we must not identify our efforts with God's reign. The reign of God always *transcends* our imperfect human attempts to embody God's values in society.

In the words of the Second Vatican Council, "the Church, by reason of her role and competence, is not identified with any political community nor bound by ties to any political system. It is at once the sign and the safeguard of the transcendental dimension of the human person." Nevertheless, it is important for the Church "to pass moral judgments even in matters relating to politics, whenever the fundamental rights of man or the salvation of souls requires it" (*Pastoral Constitution on the Church in the Modern World* [*Gaudium et Spes*], no. 76).

The ART Process of Catholic Social Teaching

Study Sheet 5, "The ART of Catholic Social Teaching," reviews the ART process. The *act* and *transform* phases of the ART process parallel the distinction between charity and justice. The task for formational and educational leaders is to engage persons in reflection that leads to both charity and justice—both to *act* to meet immediate needs and to *transform* social structures. Remember that we must help groups to learn these skills:

1. *Attend* to the situations of service before they start to *act*
2. *Research* both social data and church teaching as they *reflect*
3. *Transcend* their own efforts to *transform* society

$\mathcal{S}ession$ 2 The ART of Sharing
Catholic Social Teaching *(2 hours)*

PREPARATION—Read this sample outline and the corresponding sections of the *Leader's Guide*. For each participant, secure copies of the *Leader's Guide* or make copies of the handouts needed for this session. You may need a Bible for the prayer. Set up a registration table with name tags and a sign-in sheet. Decide ahead of time on a simple, quick way to divide the group into small groups of four to six persons. You might color-code the name tags for this purpose. Post the adopted "ground rules" from the last session for all to see. Have ready several sheets of newsprint, several markers, and a roll of masking tape. Set up the room so that the participants will be comfortable. Arrange for refreshments. Complete your setup ahead of time so that you are free to greet participants as they arrive.

INTRODUCTION—Welcome the participants. Remind them of the "Learning Objectives" (p. 12). Use the *Leader's Guide*'s introduction and Study Sheet 1, "Major Themes of Catholic Social Teaching" (p. 30), to review briefly the sources of the teaching and its seven major themes. (5 minutes)

OPENING PRAYER—Lead the group in the Prayer of Saint Francis. (They will need copies—see the "Prayers" section, p. 27.) An alternative is to have someone proclaim the Canticle of Mary (Lk 1:46-55), pausing after each verse for the group to respond, "Our spirits rejoice in God our Savior." If you select the second option, select a reader ahead of time from those who arrive early and give the person a Bible to prepare the reading. (5 minutes)

INTRODUCTIONS—Ask the participants to briefly reintroduce themselves to the group. Invite them to share their names and to name briefly one scriptural reading from their take-home assignment that spoke to them in a powerful way of the Church's social teaching. (If the group is large, you might divide them into smaller groups for introductions.) (10 minutes)

CHARITY AND JUSTICE—Use the *Leader's Guide*'s text on "Charity and Justice" (p. 12) to introduce how charity and justice are complementary but distinct. Explain the concept of social sin and the different kind of action response that it requires. Ask the participants to look over Study Sheet 4, "Charity and Justice." Use the top sections of the study sheet to summarize how charity and

15

justice complete each other and how each is unique. Then ask the group to look over the possible responses to abortion and homelessness. Ask, "How do charity and justice differ?" Give quieter members of the group an opportunity to contribute. Affirm vocal individuals and then gently redirect your attention to allow other participants to join in. (10 minutes)

SMALL GROUP DISCUSSION—Quickly divide the participants into pre-arranged small groups of four to six persons each. Briefly remind the participants of the "ground rules" from the last session. (They should be posted on newsprint for all to see.) Ask each group to develop two different lists of its own possible responses to hunger: one list for acts of charity and one for acts of justice.

Ask the small groups to be prepared to share their lists with the large group. Give each group a marker and a sheet of newsprint with a line down the middle and the headings "Charity" and "Justice" at the top of the columns. Ask them to summarize their ideas on the newsprint and to select a spokesperson to present them to the large group. Remind them of how much time they will have. (20 minutes)

REPORTS FROM SMALL GROUPS—Invite each small group to hang the newsprint with masking tape for all to see and to give a short report highlighting their ideas. To help clarify the distinction between charity and justice, at the end of each report ask if anyone has questions regarding whether an action idea is listed in the correct column. Based on their responses, draw arrows moving ideas from one column to the other if necessary. (10 minutes)

BREAK—Have refreshments available. Note the location of restrooms. (10 minutes)

THE ART OF CATHOLIC SOCIAL TEACHING—Ask the participants to look over Study Sheet 5, "The ART of Catholic Social Teaching." Use the text in the *Leader's Guide* on "The ART of Catholic Social Teaching Model" (pp. 13-14) to review the model. Note the parallels between charity and *act* in this model and the similar parallel between justice and *transform*. After presenting the model, use a few of the examples from Study Sheet 6, "Examples of the ART of Catholic Social Teaching," to illustrate the model more concretely. (10 minutes)

SMALL GROUP DISCUSSION—Form participants into the same prearranged small groups of four to six persons each. Ask each group to select a social issue—but not one of the three issues on Study Sheet 6. Other issues they might consider include poverty, lack of access to health care, refugees, migrant farm workers, euthanasia, ecology, the death penalty, and affordable child care. Ask them to use Study Sheet 7, "Using the ART of Catholic Social Teaching," to design appropriate activities for each phase of the ART model. Ask each group to be prepared to identify at least two activities for each phase of ART.

Make yourself available to them as they work. Be sure to check on each group at least once. Give each group a marker and a sheet of newsprint with two vertical lines down the length of it and the headings "Act," "Reflect," and "Transform" at the top of the columns. Ask them to summarize their ideas on the newsprint and to select a spokesperson who will present the ideas to the large group. Remind them of how much time they will have. (20 minutes)

REPORTS FROM SMALL GROUPS—Invite each small group to hang the group's newsprint with masking tape for all to see and to give a short report highlighting the ideas. To help clarify the types of activities that belong in each phase, at the end of each report ask if anyone has questions regarding whether an activity is listed in the correct column. Based on their responses, draw arrows moving ideas from one column to another if necessary. (15 minutes)

HOME STUDY—Ask the participants to use Study Sheet 6, "Examples of the ART of Catholic Social Teaching," at home in preparation for the next session. In particular, ask them to consider how activities can be adapted for different age levels. Note that the activities in each section are generally listed in order of age-appropriateness, beginning with those more suitable for younger children. Remind them of the time and place of the next meeting. Thank them for their participation. (2 minutes)

CLOSING PRAYER—Lead the group in the Prayer for Peace and Justice. (They will need copies—see the "Prayers" section, p. 27.) As an alternative, have someone proclaim Psalm 37, pausing after verses 4, 7, 11, 15, 19, 22, 26, 29, 33, 36, and 40 for the group to respond, "Trust in the Lord and do good." If you select the second option, select a reader ahead of time from those who arrive early and give the person a Bible to prepare the reading. (3 minutes)

MEETING CHECKLIST

Number of people expected: _____

X	MATERIAL/ACTION	X	MATERIAL/ACTION
	Leader's Guides		
	study sheets		
	Sharing Catholic Social Teaching books		
	name tags		
	sign-in sheet		
	newsprint		
	several markers		
	masking tape		
	Bible		
	prayer sheets		
	refreshments		
	"Ground Rules" from Session 1		

NOTES

Sharing Catholic Social Teaching

The *General Directory for Catechesis* (GDC) reminds us, "Catechesis . . . is given by right on the basis of diverse and complementary age groups, on account of the needs and capacity of its recipients" (no. 171). We need to adapt *act*, *reflect*, and *transform* (ART) activities to the age level of those with whom we minister. We must take into account their physical, emotional, intellectual, and moral maturity. These general observations will help formational leaders to take age into account in designing appropriate activities.

LEARNING OBJECTIVES
After completing this unit of study, participants will be able to do the following:

1. Identify ways to adapt social teaching activities for various ages
2. Find opportunities to link the Church's social teaching to liturgical catechesis

Physical Maturity

All persons can learn through doing. We need to respect the physical abilities and level of maturity of those with whom we work.

> ## All persons need to be emotionally engaged if they are to learn.

Younger children enjoy participating in physical activities and can learn from them. For example, art, music, dance, and outdoor activities can all be appropriate. Children can make and decorate cards, act out simple skits on social issues, or visit sites related to social justice, such as the state capital.

Older children can collect and transport food to a food shelter or engage in walk-a-thons or car washes to raise funds for worthy causes. Remember that physical coordination, strength, and stamina gradually increase with age before they gradually decline in extreme old age. (Most older adults remain in excellent health.) Be sure to consider physical requirements and safety concerns when selecting social service or social action activities. For example, it would be appropriate for high-school youth (with adult supervision and parental permission) to assist with home repairs in a low-income neighborhood, but this activity would not be appropriate for younger children.

Emotional Maturity

All persons need to be emotionally engaged if they are to learn. Persons of all ages become connected with issues when the issues take on a "human face," but we need to respect the emotional maturity of those with whom we work.

For younger age levels this emotional engagement can come through stories, puppet shows, creative play, and personal testimonies, but we must be careful to reserve more graphic presentations of emotionally intense issues for more mature audiences. The limited experience of younger children makes it possible for them to internalize fearful situations. For example, a simple exploration of hunger might rely on a child's own experience of hunger and stories of hunger in others, but it should not include graphic pictures or video clips of dying children. As the group's age level progresses, the general emotional intensity of the learning experience can increase.

Intellectual Maturity

We need to challenge all learners intellectually, but we need to reserve activities that require increasingly abstract thought for more mature persons. Younger children think concretely; the ability to think abstractly develops gradually. Not until later adolescence can persons sustain complex abstract thought. For example, it is appropriate to use simple stories or cartoons to illustrate social problems with younger children, while studying basic facts is appropriate for intermediate-age children. But analyzing social trends or statistics ought to be reserved for later ages.

Intellectual development suggests that we need to adapt the language we use in presenting the content of Catholic social teaching. Generally we move from concrete, simple language with younger persons to more abstract, complex language with older persons. And some more complex themes (e.g., workers' rights and solidarity) might be introduced later and in an initially simple form.

Presenting a comprehensive "scope and sequence" for introducing major themes and issues is beyond the purpose of this simple guide, but some examples will help to illustrate how to make age adaptations. For example, in exploring the first major theme of

Catholic social teaching (Life and Dignity of the Human Person), primary-age children might be taught that God loves everyone equally and that every person is special. Similarly, in introducing the second theme (Call to Family, Community, and Participation), younger children might spend more time on "family," since this reality is closest to their experience. Intermediate-age children might begin to explore the positive role of government in supporting families and communities. The concept of the "common good," which is more abstract, might be explored in more detail in high school and studied more intensely in college and adult education.

Younger children will not fully understand the meaning of various terms from the Catholic social tradition. Nevertheless, it is important to introduce these terms into their vocabulary as early as is appropriate and to help them to gradually deepen their understanding of the terms. We do this all the time with other religious terms. Children learn the terms "baptism" and "sin" early on, but their grasp of these realities grows throughout a lifetime.

The major themes of Catholic social teaching (Study Sheet 1) suggest many terms that ought to be known by Catholics and understood more deeply as we grow in faith, including the following: human life, human dignity, family and community, participation, the common good, human rights, the option for the poor, workers' rights, just wages, solidarity, and stewardship. As we come to know the tradition more deeply, other important terms need to become part of our vocabulary, such as subsidiarity, the sin of the world, integral human development, and the universal common good.

Of course, we cannot stop at simply helping people acquire the vocabulary of Catholic social thought. We also need to make them aware of the explicit body of Catholic social teaching and introduce them to its documents. As Catholics grow and mature, they should

> We need to make people aware of the explicit body of Catholic social teaching.

gradually be exposed to specific documents of the Church's social justice tradition. (For a bibliography, see Study Sheet 10, "Resources for the ART of Catholic Social Teaching.")

Moral Maturity

We need to respect the moral development of those with whom we work. Young children tend to make moral decisions based on the approval or disapproval of authority figures. Older children can make decisions out of respect for rules and laws. More mature persons can act out of a commitment to basic moral principles and relationships. For example, in presenting the Church's teaching on respect for human life to young children, we might appeal to the examples of Jesus and Mary; with older children we might appeal to the fifth commandment, and with more mature groups we might appeal to basic human rights.

We should inform and involve parents when we engage younger persons in social issues. This involvement respects the primary role of parents as the moral educators of their children. It is also an excellent way to engage parents with important social issues.

Our goal is to enable persons to act as moral agents. At every age we need to teach them skills and strategies so that they can apply and act on these teachings in today's world. The ART of Catholic Social Teaching offers a simple model for doing this.

Study Sheet 8, "Age Adaptations," summarizes some of the material in this section. These general observations regarding physical, emotional, intellectual, and moral maturity can help in designing age-appropriate activities. Educators and catechists will also want to draw on their own experience and on the considerable body of developmental theory and educational methodology. Persons with disabilities will bring unique strengths and needs to the educational process that will suggest further adaptations.

Adapting the ART of Catholic Social Teaching

"Examples of the ART of Catholic Social Teaching"—Study Sheet 6—can deepen the understanding of the ART process and its application to educational and formational activities. You will note that the suggested activities are generally listed in order of age-appropriateness, beginning with those more suitable for younger children. It is also true that the same activity could be done in age-appropriate ways. For example, a letter to a public official from a primary-age student could consist of a single, simple sentence expressing a concern. It might even include a drawing or picture. A letter from an older person, on the other hand, might include sophisticated arguments based on research.

OPTIONAL ACTIVITY
Pick a social issue or problem of interest to your parishioners or students. Then identify activities to help them *act*, *reflect*, and *transform* in relation to the social issue. Remember to help those with whom you work to *attend*, *research*, and *transcend* as they move through the process.

Liturgical Catechesis

The liturgical life of the Church is a rich resource for forming Catholics in the social teaching of the Church. The power of word and sacrament in the Church's liturgy should not be underestimated; it is the power of God. In the memorable words of the Second Vatican Council, "the liturgy is the summit toward which the activity of the Church is directed; it is also the fount from which all her power flows" (*Constitution on the Sacred Liturgy* [*Sacrosanctum Concilium*], no. 10).

The Church's liturgical life includes obvious catechetical opportunities such as the proclamation of God's Word and the homily, but the liturgy also forms us through sign and symbol. Liturgical catechesis and sacramental preparation need to flow in two directions: (1) prior preparation to help us to enter into the liturgical celebration at a deeper level, and (2) subsequent exploration of the experience of the liturgy to unpack its meaning for our lives.

Catechesis that prepares us for the sacraments and helps us to enter into the sacramental mysteries can form us in the Church's social teaching. Catechesis that flows from the experience of liturgy can help us gain deeper insights into the Church's social teaching. In short, liturgical catechesis can transform our world and ourselves. The *Catechism of the Catholic Church* states, "Liturgical catechesis aims to initiate people into the mystery of Christ (It is 'mystagogy.') by proceeding from the visible to the invisible, from the sign to the thing signified, from the 'sacraments' to the 'mysteries'" (no. 1075).

Earlier in this *Leader's Guide* we noted that the *Catechism* weaves Catholic social teaching throughout its text. This integration is particularly evident in part two of the *Catechism*, "The Celebration of the Christian Mystery." Catechetical and educational leaders can form persons in the social teaching of the Church through attention to liturgical celebrations, sacramental preparation (especially the sacraments of initiation), and the liturgical year. The key is to look at the social meanings of symbols and texts, not just at their personal meanings. Given our individualistic culture, this is a challenge.

Study Sheet 9, "Liturgical Catechesis and Catholic Social Teaching," explores some of the social implications of the liturgy. The sacraments of initiation (baptism, confirmation, and eucharist) are used as examples, together with examples from the liturgical year, including several major seasons, a solemnity, and a feast. Many other pointers from the Church's social teaching will occur to you as you continue to explore them in the liturgical mysteries we celebrate. Of course, it would be a mistake to focus exclusively on the social demands of the Gospel and the social

mandates of the liturgy—the personal dimension of the Gospel and the mysteries is equally important.

We need to balance both the social and the personal. We are individual persons with personal relationships and struggles. We are also social beings with communal needs and responsibilities. We bring all of this to the liturgy and gather as a community focused on entering into the paschal mystery (passion, death, resurrection, and ascension) of Jesus Christ, Savior and Lord.

Resources

Formational and educational leaders need access to a wide range of documents and programs as they share, apply, and act on the social teaching of the Church. Study Sheet 10, "Resources for the ART of Catholic Social Teaching," provides an annotated bibliography of some of the Church's major social teaching documents. This resource list also reviews programs and materials that are available through the United States Catholic Conference.

In addition to the resources listed on this study sheet, numerous associations, organizations, and publishers produce excellent educational and formational materials to help us to *reflect* on Catholic social teaching. Many other organizations offer ways to *act* in service and to *transform* unjust social structures in response to the Catholic social mission. For example, dioceses frequently sponsor homeless shelters, soup kitchens, health clinics, and other direct service programs. Many dioceses also support legislative advocacy networks and the organization of low-income communities for social change.

This *Leader's Guide* appropriately concludes with a list of resources. As leaders of education, catechesis, and formation, we need always to deepen our knowledge of Catholic social teaching. In a real sense, this simple guide is just an introduction to sharing the Church's social teaching. We are called as leaders to grow in our understanding of Catholic social teaching and to improve our skills in sharing this teaching with others.

Session 3 Sharing Catholic Social Teaching *(2 hours)*

NOTES

PREPARATION—Read this sample outline and the corresponding sections of the *Leader's Guide*. For each participant, secure copies of the *Leader's Guide* or make copies of the handouts that you will need for this session. You may need a Bible for the prayer. You will need either an easel with newsprint and a marker, a blackboard and chalk, or a melamine board and dry-erase marker. Set up a registration table with name tags and a sign-in sheet. Decide ahead of time on a simple, quick way to divide the group into small groups of four to six persons. You might color-code the name tags for this purpose. (Note that this session's groups will work on different age-level examples. See the outline below.) Post the adopted "ground rules" from the last two sessions for all to see. If possible, set up a table of resources that includes copies of the documents from Study Sheet 10 as well as brochures of local or diocesan social action programs (including legislative networks). Set up the room so that the participants will be comfortable. Arrange for refreshments. Complete your setup ahead of time so that you are free to greet participants as they arrive.

INTRODUCTION—Welcome the participants. Remind them of the "Learning Objectives" (p. 19), and use the *Leader's Guide*'s introduction and Study Sheet 1, "Major Themes of Catholic Social Teaching" (p. 30), to review briefly the sources of the teaching and its seven major themes. (5 minutes)

OPENING PRAYER—Lead the group in the "Prayer for Justice and Peace." (They will need copies—see the "Prayers" section, p. 27.) An alternative is to have someone proclaim the beatitudes (Mt 5:3-12) and pause after each verse for the group to respond, "Blessed are the poor in spirit." If you select the second option, select a reader ahead of time from those who arrive early and give the person a Bible to prepare the reading. (5 minutes)

INTRODUCTIONS—Ask the participants to reintroduce themselves briefly to the group. Invite them to share their names and to name briefly *one* insight they have gained thus far from this study of sharing Catholic social teaching. (If the group is large, you might divide participants into smaller groups for introductions.) (10 minutes)

ADAPTING THE ART OF CATHOLIC SOCIAL TEACHING WITH DIFFERENT AGE GROUPS—Briefly review the ART of Catholic Social Teaching model using Study Sheet 5. Use the *Leader's Guide*'s text on "The ART of Catholic Social Teaching Model" (pp. 13-14) to assist with this review. Emphasize the need to *attend* to the readiness of parishioners and students when using the model.

Use the *Leader's Guide*'s text on "Adapting the ART of Catholic Social Teaching" (p. 21) to explain the importance of adapting the model's activities. It will be helpful for the participants to have Study Sheet 8, "Age Adaptations," during this presentation. (15 minutes)

SMALL GROUP DISCUSSION—Divide the participants into prearranged small groups of four to six persons each. Ideally these groups should be arranged so that participants who work with persons in a given age range are together. Assign each group an age range (e.g., elementary, middle school or early adolescent, high school or later adolescent, young adult, adult, older adult). Briefly remind the participants of the "ground rules." (They should be posted on newsprint for all to see.)

Select a social issue with which all of the groups will work. Pick an issue of widespread interest to the participants. (Refer to the *Leader's Guide* and the outline of the last session for possible issues.) Ask each group to identify at least two age-appropriate activities for each of the three phases of the ART process. Ask them to be prepared to share their lists with the large group. Each group needs to select a spokesperson to present the ideas to the large group. Remind them of how much time they will have. (20 minutes)

BREAK—Have refreshments available. Note location of restrooms. Invite them to browse the resource table. You might have resources available for them to borrow—if so, have a sign-out sheet. (10 minutes)

REPORTS FROM SMALL GROUPS—This time, conduct the small group reports in a "round-robin" style. Starting with ideas for the *act* phase of ART only, ask each small group—beginning with those working with the youngest ages—to briefly describe their ideas. This procedure should concretely illustrate age adaptations. After all groups have reported, begin another round for *reflect* activities and then a third for *transform* activities. Remind spokespersons to be brief. (15 minutes)

LITURGICAL CATECHESIS—Use the text in the *Leader's Guide* on "Liturgical Catechesis" (pp. 21-22) to describe how the liturgical life of the Church is a rich resource for forming Catholics in the social teaching of the Church. (10 minutes)

MAKING LINKS—Ask the participants to look over Study Sheet 9, "Liturgical Catechesis and Catholic Social Teaching." Remind the participants that in this study we focus exclusively on the social implications of the Gospel and the Church's liturgy but that the personal dimension is important as well. On newsprint, blackboard, or melamine board, make three columns. Write these headings above the columns: "Liturgical Element," "Link to Social Teaching," and "Social Issue." Ask the participants to name other liturgical celebrations, rites, or observances. As each is named, ask the group to name a "link" to the *social* teaching of the Church (perhaps a theme) and then to identify contemporary social issues related to this link. Fill in the other two columns.

An alternative method of exploring these connections is to have the group look over Study Sheet 9 and suggest additional links and issues for the liturgical elements presented on the sheet.

Give quieter members of the group an opportunity to contribute. Affirm vocal individuals and then gently redirect your attention to allow other participants to join in. (15 minutes)

HOME STUDY—Use the description of "Resources" on p. 22 and review with the participants Study Sheet 10, "Resources for the ART of Catholic Social Teaching." Invite them to browse the resource table again after the session. If they can borrow materials, make the sign-out sheet available. Thank them for their participation. Encourage them to continue to deepen their knowledge of Catholic social teaching and to improve their skills in sharing it with others. (10 minutes)

CLOSING PRAYER—Lead the group in praying Archbishop Oscar Romero's reflection "Prophets of a Future not Our Own." (They will need copies—see the "Prayers" section, p. 28.) You might instead have someone read Romero's reflection to the group, pausing after each paragraph for the group to respond, "We are prophets of a future not our own." Or if you prefer, use one of the other prayers or scriptural readings from an earlier session, or design another prayer experience. If you select a scriptural option, select a reader ahead of time from those who arrive early and give the person a Bible to prepare the reading. (5 minutes)

MEETING CHECKLIST

Number of people expected:_____

X	MATERIAL/ACTION	X	MATERIAL/ACTION
	Leader's Guides		
	study sheets		
	Sharing Catholic Social Teaching books		
	name tags		
	sign-in sheet		
	newsprint, blackboard, or melamine board		
	marker, chalk, or dry-erase marker		
	Bible		
	prayer sheets		
	refreshments		
	"Ground Rules" from Session 1		
	resources for table		

NOTES

Prayers

Prayer of Saint Francis

Lord make me an instrument of your peace,
Where there is hatred let me sow love.
Where there is injury, pardon.
Where there is doubt, faith.
Where there is despair, hope.
Where there is darkness, light.
And where there is sadness, joy.
O Divine Master, grant that I may
not so much seek to be consoled as to console;
to be understood as to understand;
To be loved as to love.
For it is in giving that we receive.
It is in pardoning that we are pardoned.
And it is in dying that we are born to eternal life.
Amen.

Prayer for Peace and Justice

God, source of all light,
We are surrounded by the darkness of
the injustices experienced by your people,
the poor who are hungry and who search
for shelter, the sick who seek relief,
and the downtrodden who seek help in
their hopelessness.

Surround us and fill us with your Spirit
who is Light.
Lead us in your way to be light to your people.
Help our parish to be salt for our community
as we share your love with those caught
in the struggles of life.

We desire to be your presence to the least
among us
and to know your presence in them as we
work through you
to bring justice and peace to this world
in desperate need.

We ask this through our Lord Jesus Christ,
your Son, who lives and reigns with you
and the Holy Spirit, one God, for ever and ever.
Amen.

—United States Catholic Conference, Department of Social Development and World Peace, *Communities of Salt and Light: Parish Resource Manual* (Washington, D.C.: United States Catholic Conference, 1994), p. 48

Prophets of a Future Not Our Own

BY ARCHBISHOP OSCAR ROMERO

(Archbishop Oscar Romero championed the rights of the poor in El Salvador and called for an end to the violence and injustices that plagued his nation during its bloody civil war. He was martyred at the altar on March 24, 1980, for his defense of the poor. His words make a fitting closing reflection for this unit of study.)

It helps, now and then, to step back and take the
    long view.
The kingdom is not only beyond our efforts, it is
    beyond our vision.
We accomplish in our lifetime only a tiny fraction of
    the magnificent enterprise that is God's work.
Nothing we do is complete, which is another way of
    saying that the kingdom always lies beyond us.
No statement says all that could be said.
No prayer fully expresses our faith.
No confession brings perfection.
No pastoral visit brings wholeness.

No program accomplishes the Church's mission.
No set of goals and objectives includes everything.
This is what we are about:
We plant seeds that one day will grow.
We water seeds already planted, knowing that they
    hold future promise.
We lay foundations that will need further develop-
    ment.
We provide yeast that produces effects beyond our
    capabilities.
We cannot do everything
and there is a sense of liberation in realizing that.
This enables us to do something,
and to do it very well.
It may be incomplete, but it is a beginning, a step
    along the way,
an opportunity for God's grace to enter and do the
    rest.
We may never see the end results,
but that is the difference between the master builder
    and the worker.
We are workers, not master builders,
ministers, not messiahs.
We are prophets of a future not our own.
Amen.

Leader's Guide to
Sharing
Catholic Social Teaching
Session Study Sheets

Study Sheet 1
Major Themes of Catholic Social Teaching

1. LIFE AND DIGNITY OF THE HUMAN PERSON

"Our belief in the sanctity of human life and the inherent dignity of the human person is the foundation of all the principles of our social teaching." Every person is created in the image of God. Every person is precious. All social laws, practices, and institutions must protect, not undermine, human life and human dignity—from conception through natural death.

2. CALL TO FAMILY, COMMUNITY, AND PARTICIPATION

"How we organize our society—in economics and politics, in law and policy—directly affects human dignity and the capacity of individuals to grow in community." We are social beings. We realize our dignity and human potential in our families and communities. The family is the basic cell of society; it must be supported. Government has the mission of protecting human life, promoting the common good of all persons, and defending the right and duty of all to participate in social life.

3. RIGHTS AND RESPONSIBILITIES

"The Catholic tradition teaches that human dignity can be protected and a healthy community can be achieved only if human rights are protected and responsibilities are met." The Church upholds both personal responsibility and social rights. The right to life is fundamental and includes a right to food, clothing, shelter, rest, medical care, and essential social services. Every person has the right to raise a family and the duty to support them. Human dignity demands religious and political freedom and the duty to exercise these rights for the common good of all persons.

4. OPTION FOR THE POOR AND VULNERABLE

"Catholic teaching proclaims that a basic moral test is how our most vulnerable members are faring." The Church does not pit one social group against another but instead follows the example of our Lord, who identified himself with the poor and the vulnerable (cf. Mt 25:31-46). Giving priority concern to the poor and the vulnerable strengthens the health of the whole society. The human life and dignity of the poor are most at risk. The poor have the first claim on our personal and social resources.

5. THE DIGNITY OF WORK AND THE RIGHTS OF WORKERS

"Work is more than a way to make a living; it is a form of continuing participation in God's creation." Workers have rights to decent work, just wages, safe working conditions, unionization, disability protection, retirement security, and economic initiative. The economy exists for the human person; the human person does not exist for the economy. Labor has priority over capital.

6. SOLIDARITY

"We are one human family, whatever our national, racial, ethnic, economic, and ideological differences." The Church speaks of a "universal" common good that reaches beyond our nation's borders to the global community. Solidarity recognizes that the fates of the peoples of the earth are linked. Solidarity requires richer nations to aid poorer ones, commands respect for different cultures, demands justice in international relationships, and calls on all nations to live in peace with one another.

7. CARE FOR GOD'S CREATION

"We show our respect for the Creator by our stewardship of creation." Good stewardship of the earth and of all its creatures (including human beings) is a complex challenge. Humans are part of creation itself, and whatever we do to the earth we ultimately do to ourselves. We must live in harmony with the rest of creation and preserve it for future generations.

These quotations are from the U.S. Catholic bishops' statement *Sharing Catholic Social Teaching: Challenges and Directions* (Washington, D.C.: United States Catholic Conference, 1998), pp. 4-6. The summary of these themes also draws from statements of the U.S. Catholic bishops on *A Century of Social Teaching* (1991) and *Political Responsibility: Proclaiming the Gospel of Life, Protecting the Least Among Us, and Pursuing the Common Good* (1995), as well as from other church documents.

Study Sheet 2
Quotes from Official Church Documents

1. LIFE AND DIGNITY OF THE HUMAN PERSON

"All offenses against life itself, such as murder, geno-cide, abortion, euthanasia and wilful suicide; all viola-tions of the integrity of the human person . . . all offenses against human dignity, such as subhuman liv-ing conditions, arbitrary imprisonment, deportation, slavery, prostitution, the selling of women and chil-dren, degrading working conditions where men are treated as mere tools for profit rather than free and responsible persons: all these and the like are criminal: they poison civilization . . . and militate against the honor of the creator."

—Second Vatican Council, *Pastoral Constitution on the Church in the Modern World* (*Gaudium et Spes*), no. 27

"Every individual, precisely by reason of the mystery of the Word of God who was made flesh (cf. Jn 1:14), is entrusted to the maternal care of the Church. There-fore every threat to human dignity and life must nec-essarily be felt in the Church's very heart; it cannot but affect her at the core of her faith in the Redemp-tive Incarnation of the Son of God, and engage her in her mission of proclaiming the *Gospel of life* in all the world and to every creature (cf. Mk 16:15)."

—Pope John Paul II, *The Gospel of Life* (*Evangelium Vitae*), no. 3

2. CALL TO FAMILY, COMMUNITY, AND PARTICIPATION

"It is necessary that all participate, each according to his position and role, in promoting the common good. This obligation is inherent in the dignity of the human person. Participation is achieved first of all by taking charge of the areas for which one assumes personal responsibility. . . . As far as possible, citizens should take an active part in *public life*."

—*Catechism of the Catholic Church*, nos. 1913-1915

"One must pay tribute to those nations whose systems permit the largest possible number of the citizens to take part in public life in a climate of genuine freedom. . . ."

—Second Vatican Council, *Pastoral Constitution on the Church in the Modern World* (*Gaudium et Spes*), no. 31

"It is necessary to go back to seeing the family as the sanctuary of life. The family is indeed sacred: it is the place in which life—the gift of God—can be properly welcomed and protected against the many attacks to which it is exposed, and can develop in accordance with what constitutes authentic human growth. In the face of the so-called culture of death, the family is the heart of the culture of life."

—Pope John Paul II, *On the Hundredth Anniversary of Rerum Novarum* (*Centesimus Annus*), no. 39

3. RIGHTS AND RESPONSIBILITIES

"It is not right . . . for either the citizen or the family to be absorbed by the state; it is proper that the indi-vidual and the family should be permitted to retain their freedom of action, so far as this is possible without jeopardizing the common good and without injuring anyone."

—Pope Leo XIII, *On the Condition of Workers* (*Rerum Novarum*), no. 52

"[The State] has also the duty to protect the rights of all its people, and particularly of its weaker members, the workers, women and children. It can never be right for the State to shirk its obligation to work actively for the betterment of the condition of [workers]."

—Pope John XXIII, *On Christianity and Social Progress* (*Mater et Magistra*), no. 20

"Beginning our discussion of the rights of man, we see that every man has the right to life, to bodily integrity, and to the means which are suitable for the proper development of life; these are primarily food, clothing, shelter, rest, medical care, and finally the necessary social services. Therefore a human being also has the right to security in cases of sickness, inability to work, widowhood, old age, unemployment, or in any other case in which he is deprived of the means of subsis-tence through no fault of his own."

—Pope John XXIII, *Peace on Earth* (*Pacem in Terris*), no. 11

"[The Catholic tradition calls for] *a society of free work, of enterprise and of participation*. Such a society is not directed against the market, but demands that the market be appropriately controlled by the forces of society and by the State, so as to guarantee that the basic needs of the whole of society are satisfied."

—Pope John Paul II, *On the Hundredth Anniversary of Rerum Novarum (Centesimus Annus)*, no. 35

4. OPTION FOR THE POOR AND VULNERABLE

"In protecting the rights of private individuals . . . special consideration must be given to the weak and the poor. For the nation, as it were, of the rich, is guarded by its own defenses and is in less need of governmental protection. . . ."

—Pope Leo XIII, *On the Condition of Workers (Rerum Novarum)*, no. 54

"The prime purpose of this special commitment to the poor is to enable them to become active participants in the life of society. It is to enable *all* persons to share in and contribute to the common good. The 'option for the poor,' therefore, is not an adversarial slogan that pits one group or class against another. Rather it states that the deprivation and powerlessness of the poor wounds the whole community. The extent of their suffering is a measure of how far we are from being a true community of persons. These wounds will be healed only by greater solidarity with the poor and among the poor themselves."

—National Conference of Catholic Bishops, *Economic Justice For All*, no. 88

5. THE DIGNITY OF WORK AND THE RIGHTS OF WORKERS

"We must first of all recall a principle that has always been taught by the Church: the principle of the priority of labor over capital. This principle directly concerns the process of production: In this process labor is always a primary efficient cause, while capital, the whole collection of means of production, remains a mere instrument or instrumental cause."

—Pope John Paul II, *On Human Work (Laborem Exercens)*, no. 12

"All people have the right to economic initiative, to productive work, to just wages and benefits, to decent working conditions, as well as to organize and join unions or other associations."

—National Conference of Catholic Bishops, *A Catholic Framework for Economic Life*, no. 5

6. SOLIDARITY

"This moreover must be repeated: what is superfluous in richer regions must serve the needs of the regions in want. . . . Their avarice if continued will call down the punishment of God and arouse the anger of the poor. . . ."

—Pope Paul VI, *On the Development of Peoples (Populorum Progressio)*, no. 49

"Because peace, like the kingdom of God itself, is both a divine gift and a human work, the Church should continually pray for the gift and share in the work. We are called to be a Church at the service of peace, precisely because peace is one manifestation of God's word and work in our midst."

—National Conference of Catholic Bishops, *The Challenge of Peace: God's Promise and Our Response*, no. 23

"Interdependence must be transformed into *solidarity*, based upon the principle that the goods of creation *are meant for all*. That which human industry produces through the processing of raw materials, with the contribution of work, must serve equally for the good of all. . . .

"*Solidarity* helps us to see the 'other'—whether a *person, people or nation*—not just as some kind of instrument, with a work capacity and physical strength to be exploited at low cost and then discarded when no longer useful, but as our 'neighbor,' a 'helper,' to be made a sharer, on a par with ourselves, in the banquet of life to which all are equally invited by God."

—Pope John Paul II, *On Social Concern (Sollicitudo Rei Socialis)*, no. 39

7. CARE FOR GOD'S CREATION

"The dominion granted to man by the Creator is not an absolute power, nor can one speak of a freedom to 'use and misuse,' or to dispose of things as one pleases. The limitation imposed from the beginning by the Creator himself . . . shows clearly enough that, when it comes to the natural world, we are subject not only to biological laws but also to moral ones, which cannot be violated with impunity."

—Pope John Paul II, *On Social Concern (Sollicitudo Rei Socialis)*, no. 34

"At its core, the environmental crisis is a moral challenge. It calls us to examine how we use and share the goods of the earth, what we pass on to future generations, and how we live in harmony with God's creation."

—National Conference of Catholic Bishops, *Renewing the Earth: An Invitation to Reflection and Action on Environment in Light of Catholic Social Teaching*, p. 1

Study Sheet 3
Some Scriptural Foundations of Catholic Social Teaching

For each theme read a few of the passages cited. Consider how the scriptural passage reflects the theme.

1. LIFE AND DIGNITY OF THE HUMAN PERSON

Every social decision and institution must be judged in light of whether it protects or undermines the life and dignity of the human person.

- Genesis 1:26-27 (created in the image of God)
- Deuteronomy 30:19 (choose life)
- Psalm 8:5-7 (humans made little less than a god)
- John 12:32 (Christ will draw all to himself)
- 1 Corinthians 15:22 (Christ died for all)

2. CALL TO FAMILY, COMMUNITY, AND PARTICIPATION

Human dignity can be realized and protected only in community.

- Genesis 17:7-8 (God covenants with a people)
- Exodus 6:6-8 (God's covenant frees a people)
- Leviticus 19:9-15, 35-37; Deuteronomy 14:22-29, 15:1-18, 24:10-22 (some of covenant's social laws)
- Jeremiah 32:38-40 (God's covenant with a people and their children)
- Mark 1:14-15 (the reign of God, a social image)
- Luke 22:14-20; 1 Corinthians 11:23-26; Hebrews 8:7-12 (Christ's new covenant)

3. HUMAN RIGHTS AND RESPONSIBILITIES

Catholic social teaching recognizes three sets of rights: the right to life (including food and shelter), economic rights (including education and employment), and political and cultural rights (including religious freedom). With rights come responsibilities to others, to our families, and to the common good of all.

- Deuteronomy 5:17, 30:19 (right to life)
- Sirach 34:22 (rights of workers)
- Psalm 146:5-8 (freedom from oppression)
- Isaiah 10:1-2 (against unjust laws)

4. OPTION FOR THE POOR AND VULNERABLE

All members of society and society as a whole have a special obligation to poor and vulnerable persons. God's covenant includes a special concern for these persons.

- Exodus 22:20-22; Leviticus 19:33-34; Deuteronomy 24:17-18 (laws protecting aliens, widows, orphans)
- Exodus 22:24-26; Leviticus 25:23-28; Deuteronomy 15:1-11, 23:20, 24:6 and 10-13 (laws protecting debtors)
- Deuteronomy 14:28-29, 26:12-13 (laws providing for the poor)
- Matthew 25:31-46 (judgment of nations)
- Luke 4:16-21 (Jesus' mission to the poor/outcast)
- Luke 14:12-14 (reach out to the poor/vulnerable)

©Virginia Broderick

> # With rights come responsibilities to others, to our families, and to the common good of all.

5. THE DIGNITY OF WORK AND THE RIGHTS OF WORKERS

Human dignity finds special expression in the dignity of work and in the rights of workers. Through work we participate in creation. Workers have rights to just wages, rest, and fair working conditions.

- Genesis 2:2-3 (God labors and rests)
- Genesis 2:15 (humans cultivate earth)
- Exodus 20:9-11, 23:12, 34:21; Leviticus 23:3; Deuteronomy 5:12-15 (Sabbath gave laborers rest)
- Leviticus 19:13; Deuteronomy 24:14-15; Sirach 34:22; Jeremiah 22:13; James 5:4 (wage justice)
- Isaiah 58:3 (do not drive laborers)
- Matthew 20:1-16 (Jesus uses wage law in parable)
- Mark 6:3 (Jesus worked as carpenter)
- Mark 2:27 (Sabbath is for benefit of people)
- Matthew 10:9-10; Luke 10:7; 1 Timothy 5:17-18 (laborer deserves pay)

6. SOLIDARITY

We are called to global solidarity. We are one human family regardless of national, racial, ethnic, gender, economic, or ideological boundaries. Global solidarity expresses concerns for world peace and international development.

- Genesis 22:17-18; Psalm 22:28-29 (save all nations)
- Isaiah 2:1-4; Micah 4:1-3 (peace for all nations)
- Romans 10:12 (no national distinctions in God)
- Galatians 3:28 (all one in Christ)

7. CARE FOR GOD'S CREATION

Our faith calls us to be good stewards of the earth and all its creatures.

- Genesis 1:31 (goodness of creation)
- Genesis 2:15 (stewardship of earth)
- Daniel 3:74-81 (all the earth blesses God)
- Hosea 4:1-3 (humans wound the earth)
- Romans 8:18-25 (all creation awaits redemption)

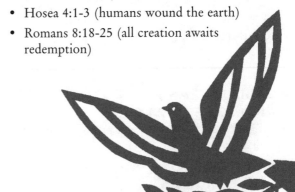

Study Sheet 4
Charity and Justice

1. Use the top sections of this table to reflect on how charity and justice complete one another and on how each is unique.
2. Next look at the possible responses to abortion and homelessness. How do they differ?
3. Finally, write down some possible ways to work on the issue of hunger. In the first column limit yourself to acts of charity; in the second column limit yourself to acts of justice.

	CHARITY	JUSTICE
GENERAL RESPONSES	Focuses on the needs of individuals, families, and all creation Looks at individual situations Meets an immediate need Addresses painful individual symptoms of social problems Relies on the generosity of donors	Focuses on the rights of individuals, families, and all creation Analyzes social situations or social structures Works for long-term social change Addresses the underlying social causes of individual problems Relies on just laws and fair social structures
RESPONSES TO ABORTION	Give women alternatives to abortion, including adoption. Provide prenatal care and medical services for poor women. Offer crisis pregnancy services, especially to unwed mothers.	Extend legal protection to unborn children. Reform health care system to make medical care accessible to all. Adopt pro-family public policies that help families with children.
RESPONSES TO HOMELESSNESS	Shelter homeless persons. Find jobs for homeless persons. Provide emergency assistance to prevent evictions.	Reduce housing costs through tax credits or low-income housing. Increase wages of working poor to make housing affordable. Reform laws to protect tenants' rights and enforce building codes.
POSSIBLE RESPONSES TO HUNGER		

Study Sheet 5
The ART of Catholic Social Teaching

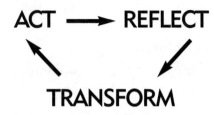

ACT ⟶ REFLECT

TRANSFORM

> Action on behalf of justice and participation in the transformation of the world fully appear to us as a constitutive dimension of the preaching to the Gospel, or, in other Words, of the Church's mission for the redemption of the human race and its liberation from every oppressive situation.
>
> —World Synod of Bishops, *Justice in the World,* in *Justice in the Marketplace* (Washington, D.C.: United States Catholic Conference, 1985), p. 250

ACT	REFLECT	TRANSFORM
. . . to meet immediate and urgent needs. (charity)	**. . . on root causes and Catholic social teaching.**	**. . . the root social causes. (justice)**
Act to alleviate the symptoms of social problems. Examples: Feed the hungry, shelter the homeless, resettle refugees, protect victims of domestic violence, and collect recyclables. Come in contact with the issue; allow it to take on a face. Perform the **Corporal Works of Mercy:** • Feed the hungry. • Give drink to the thirsty. • Clothe the naked. • Shelter the homeless. • Visit the imprisoned. • Visit the sick. • Bury the dead. (See Matthew 25 and Tobit 2.)	Ask, **"Why?"** Why are people hungry, homeless, uprooted, battered or discriminated against? **Why** is our ecosystem deteriorating? Listen to those who are most directly affected: the poor and the marginalized. Ask deeper questions that challenge the status quo. Explore the underlying causes of poverty, violence, homelessness, racism, ecological devastation, and other issues. What does Scripture and Catholic social teaching say about these social issues and their causes?	**Transform** the social structures that contribute to suffering and injustice. To **transform** is to take a different kind of action. **Transformative action** gets at the root causes; it does not stop at alleviating symptoms. **Transform** our communities and our world through • advocating for just laws and public policies • working with organized low-income people • patronizing or boycotting businesses based on social values • living simply and ecologically • investing in socially responsible ways • creating new social structures (e.g., low-income housing)
ATTEND to both the readiness of parishioners and students to serve and to the dignity of the poor.	Do **RESEARCH** in the social sciences, with those affected by the issue, and in Catholic social teaching.	**TRANSCEND** political and social ideologies and do not identify specific initiatives with God's reign.

Study Sheet 6

Examples of the ART
of Catholic Social Teaching

Study the following examples of activities that apply the ART of Catholic Social Teaching framework to violence, homelessness, and global hunger. Pick another social issue of interest to your learners, and identify age-appropriate ART activities that will involve parishioners or students.

ISSUE	ACT	REFLECT	TRANSFORM
VIOLENCE	• Reach out to a family who has suffered a violent crime, providing food. • Raise funds or collect food, clothing, and toys for a domestic violence shelter. • Volunteer at a shelter. • Send aid to a community rebuilding after a war. • Visit a hospitalized crime victim or a prisoner. • Help a refugee family fleeing conflict to resettle. • Train leaders and teachers to identify domestic violence.	• Explore children's relationships and causes of fights. • Study the fifth commandment and the beatitudes. • Plan a parents' meeting on media violence and children. • Read *Confronting a Culture of Violence*, by the U.S. bishops. • Learn about domestic violence and church teaching on it. • Study the root causes of violent crime (e.g., poverty, substance abuse, racism). • Reflect on the U.S. bishops' *The Challenge of Peace: God's Promise and Our Response.*	• Write letters to legislators about the violence of abortion, capital punishment, or the arms race. • Institute a faculty and student pledge to reject violent language and behaviors. • Sponsor nonviolent conflict resolution training for students or parents. • Organize a parish or school media boycott of violent programs and advertisers. • Support programs to assist inmates' return to society.
HOMELESSNESS	• Prepare cards or table decorations for a homeless feeding program. • Collect food, clothing, or funds for a local shelter. • Volunteer to serve a meal at a shelter. • Raise funds for emergency assistance programs to prevent evictions by paying rents. • Support job training and placement for able homeless persons.	• Review the Christmas narratives, noting how Joseph and Mary sought shelter. Why do we need a home? • Study surveys of homelessness in your area. Pay close attention to its causes. • Reflect on the Church's social teaching on housing as a basic human right. • Learn about the Catholic Campaign for Human Development (CCHD).	• Raise funds to build low-income housing. • Contact legislators about low-cost housing and tax credits for the working poor. • Support a living wage ordinance and businesses that pay a living wage. • Support housing rehabilitation programs. • Support a CCHD project to empower homeless persons or families.
GLOBAL HUNGER	• Contribute funds for children in need through the Holy Childhood Association (HCA). • Connect Lenten practices to overseas hunger through Catholic Relief Service's (CRS) Operation Rice Bowl. • Conduct a "food fast" retreat. Donate funds to CRS. • Collect medical or school supplies for children overseas. • Support twinning projects between your parish and a Third World community.	• Study bible stories about hunger and our own needs for food. • Show a CRS film on global hunger or poverty. • Study the causes of hunger, including the arms trade and need for land reform. • Review church teaching on food as a basic human right stemming from the right to life. Study specific documents. • Write a letter to the editor urging more coverage of hunger issues.	• Fund a CRS development project in the Third World. • Write Congress about the need to cut foreign military aid and to increase global development assistance. • Host a craft fair featuring crafts made overseas and sold at fair prices. Contact CRS. • Support land reform initiatives in the Third World to give the poor access to farmland.

Study Sheet 7
Using the ART of Catholic Social Teaching

ACT ⟶ REFLECT

↖ ↙

TRANSFORM

Social Issue:

ACT	REFLECT	TRANSFORM
. . . to meet immediate and urgent needs. (charity)	. . . on root causes and Catholic social teaching.	. . . the root social causes. (justice)

Study Sheet 8
Age Adaptations

This study sheet suggests some things to consider when adapting act, reflect, and transform activities for different age groups.

PHYSICAL

All people learn through doing. Respect the physical abilities of those with whom we work.

- Young children love to learn through physical activity.
- In general, physical coordination, strength, and stamina gradually increase with age.

EMOTIONAL

All people need to be emotionally engaged to learn. Issues need to take on a human face.

- Young children can be engaged emotionally through storytelling.
- The ability to handle intense emotional experiences generally increases with age.

INTELLECTUAL

Younger persons think concretely; the ability to think abstractly develops gradually.

- The language of Catholic social teaching needs to be adapted: simple, concrete language for younger children; more abstract, complex language for more mature persons.
- Catholics need to acquire the vocabulary of Catholic social teaching.

- Basic terms of Catholic social teaching need to be introduced as early as appropriate; as persons mature, they need to deepen their understandings of these terms.
- As Catholics grow and mature, they should be exposed to documents of the Church's social teaching.

MORAL

We need to respect the moral development of those with whom we work.

- Young children tend to make moral decisions based on the approval or disapproval of authority figures.
- Older children can make decisions out of respect for rules and laws.
- Children rely on their parents for moral guidance; we should involve parents when we engage younger persons in social issues.
- More mature persons can act out of a commitment to basic moral principles and relationships.

These general observations can help when adapting activities to various age groups. Developmental and educational research can provide a wealth of additional insights. Remember that persons with disabilities will have unique strengths and needs.

Study Sheet 9
Liturgical Catechesis and Catholic Social Teaching

Review these selected liturgical elements and their links to the Church's social teaching and social issues. The examples read across. Can you think of other examples?

LITURGY	LITURGICAL ELEMENTS	CATHOLIC SOCIAL TEACHING LINKS	POSSIBLE ISSUES TO EXPLORE
BAPTISM AND CONFIRMATION	Exorcisms	Rejection of "the sin of the world" or "structures of sin"	Social laws/realities that violate human life and dignity
	Blessing of Baptismal Water	Passing through waters of Red Sea places us on journey from slavery to freedom (human rights)	Respect for basic human rights (e.g., religious freedom, immigration, non-discrimination)
	Baptism with Water	Water: symbol of new birth and life; essential to all life (care of the earth)	Respect for life (abortion, euthanasia, capital punishment); ecology
	Reception of the Lighted Candle	Light: symbol of our mission to be "the light of the world"	Our mission is to enlighten debates of public and corporate policies
	Anointing with Sacred Chrism	Anointed to "bring glad tidings to the poor, release to captives" (Lk 4:18)	Called to take up Christ's mission to world with all its social implications
EUCHARISTIC CELEBRATION	Penitential Rite	Participation in "the sin of the world" or "structures of sin"	Unjust laws, social prejudices, unfair business practices
	Liturgy of the Word	See Study Sheet 3 ("Some Scriptural Foundations") for examples	Address the full range of the Church's social concerns
	Creed	Faith in "one God" recognizes unity and dignity of all people	Global solidarity, racism, ethnic cleansing, war and peace
	Offertory	Gifts for those in need remind us of the option for the poor	Poverty, living wages, health care, international development
	Communion Rite	The Body of Christ commits us to the poor; sharing bread with all	Hunger (worldwide); unity of human family (solidarity, world peace)
	Sign of Peace	The peace of Christ calls us to be peace for one another	World peace, arms trade, solidarity, violence
	Concluding Rite	Sent forth in mission to the world; "Mass" (Latin *missa*, to send)	Our mission is to act on social teaching in families, work, public
LITURGICAL YEAR	Advent	Expectation of Messiah; preparation for the reign of God	Building a society that mirrors values of reign of God, Prince of Peace
	Christmas	Incarnation divinizes humanity and affirms human dignity	Human life and dignity; human rights
	Feast of the Holy Innocents	This slaughter highlights need to protect vulnerable children	Abortion, child abuse, childhood hunger and disease
	Lent	Penitential prayer, almsgiving, fasting; solidarity with poor	Poverty, world hunger, global development, simple lifestyle
	Easter Season	The risen Lord conquers death and enters into his reign	Issues of life and death; example of early Church's serving the poor
	Solemnity of Christ the King	Nothing lies outside the scope of Christ's concern or mission	All political, social, and cultural forces are accountable to God
	Memorial of Francis of Assisi	Simplicity of life and poverty call us to live in harmony with nature	Care of God's creation and option for the poor

Study Sheet 10
Resources for the ART
of Catholic Social Teaching

Papal Social Teaching

(CHRONOLOGICAL ORDER)

Pope Leo XIII. *On the Condition of Workers (Rerum Novarum)*. 1891. In *Contemporary Catholic Social Teaching*. Washington, D.C.: United States Catholic Conference, 1991.

This foundational document marks the beginning of modern Catholic social teaching. Pope Leo addresses the plight of workers, rejects class struggle, affirms workers' rights, and supports unions.

Pope Pius XI. *On Reconstructing the Social Order (Quadragesimo Anno)*. 1931. In *Contemporary Catholic Social Teaching*. Washington, D.C.: United States Catholic Conference, 1991.

This encyclical denounces the concentration of wealth and economic power and calls for the reconstruction of the social order based on subsidiarity. Pope Pius XI commemorates the fortieth anniversary of *Rerum Novarum*.

Pope John XXIII. *On Christianity and Social Progress (Mater et Magistra)*. 1961. In *Proclaiming Justice and Peace: Papal Documents from "Rerum Novarum" Through "Centesimus Annus."* Rev. ed. Mystic, Conn.: Twenty-Third Publications, 1991.

Seventy years after *Rerum Novarum*, Pope John XXIII affirms the role of the Church as a social teacher. He expresses profound concerns for the growing gap between rich and poor nations, for the plight of farmers and rural areas, and for the arms race.

Pope John XXIII. *Peace on Earth (Pacem in Terris)*. 1963. Washington, D.C.: United States Catholic Conference, 1963.

In this encyclical, Pope John XXIII affirms human rights, calls for peace based on trust and respect for these rights, urges disarmament, and supports creation of a world authority to protect the universal common good.

Pope Paul VI. *On the Development of Peoples (Populorum Progressio)*. 1967. Washington, D.C.: United States Catholic Conference, 1967.

Saying that the world's poor are marginalized, Pope Paul VI calls for integral human development, criticizes unjust economic structures that lead to inequality, and calls for new international economic and social relationships.

Pope Paul VI. *A Call to Action: On the Occasion of the Eightieth Anniversary of the Encyclical Rerum Novarum (Octogesima Adveniens)*. 1971. In *Justice in the Marketplace*. Washington, D.C.: United States Catholic Conference, 1985.

Marking the eightieth anniversary of *Rerum Novarum*, Pope Paul VI asks Christians to work for social and political reform to promote social justice. He affirms the role of individuals and local Christian communities in overcoming injustices.

Pope Paul VI. *On Evangelization in the Modern World (Evangelii Nuntiandi)*. 1975. Washington, D.C.: United States Catholic Conference, 1975.

Pope Paul VI articulates a "new evangelization" that links social transformation with the proclamation of the Gospel. In light of many social challenges, he calls for an evangelization that transforms both individual believers and social structures.

Pope John Paul II. *Redeemer of Man (Redemptor Hominis)*. 1979. Washington, D.C.: United States Catholic Conference, 1979.

In his first encyclical, Pope John Paul II examines human dignity and rights in light of the mystery of redemption. He questions the adequacy of current economic and political structures to address injustices.

Pope John Paul II. *On Human Work* (*Laborem Exercens*). 1981. Washington, D.C.: United States Catholic Conference, 1981.

On the ninetieth anniversary of *Rerum Novarum*, Pope John Paul II defends the dignity of work and the rights of workers. He explores just wages and the right to organize, and he affirms the priority of labor over capital.

Pope John Paul II. *On Social Concern* (*Sollicitudo Rei Socialis*). 1987. Washington, D.C.: United States Catholic Conference, 1987.

Pope John Paul II reaffirms the tradition of the Church's social teaching. He critiques East-West blocs and other "structures of sin" that compromise the progress of poor nations. The pope calls for solidarity between rich and poor nations.

Pope John Paul II. *On the Hundredth Anniversary of Rerum Novarum* (*Centesimus Annus*). 1991. Washington, D.C.: United States Catholic Conference, 1991.

Pope John Paul II observes the centennial of *Rerum Novarum*, examining the failure of communism and the limitations of capitalism. He restates themes of Pope Leo's encyclical and calls for a just society based on rights of workers, economic initiative, and participation.

Pope John Paul II. *The Gospel of Life* (*Evangelium Vitae*). 1995. Washington, D.C.: United States Catholic Conference, 1995.

Pope John Paul II explores threats to human life and signs of hopefulness. He decries the culture of death and calls for a culture of life. The encyclical names a wide range of old and new life issues but concentrates on newer threats.

Conciliar and Synodal

(CHRONOLOGICAL ORDER)

Second Vatican Council. *Pastoral Constitution on the Church in the Modern World* (*Gaudium et Spes*). 1965. In Austin Flannery, ed. *Vatican Council II: The Conciliar and Post Conciliar Documents*. New rev. ed. Northport, N.Y.: Costello Publishing Company, 1996.

The council engages the Church with the challenges of modern society. The document explores social teaching, addresses a wide range of social issues, and

calls on all Christians to act in defense of human life, human dignity, and peace.

World Synod of Bishops. *Justice in the World*. 1971. In *Justice in the Marketplace*. Washington, D.C.: United States Catholic Conference, 1985.

This document locates action for justice at the heart of the Gospel (as "constitutive") and calls on the Church itself to be just if it would venture to speak to others about justice.

General Resources

Catechism of the Catholic Church. Washington, D.C.: United States Catholic Conference, 1994.

This integrates Catholic social teaching throughout its text and includes a major treatment of social teaching and various social issues in part three, "Life in Christ."

Congregation for the Clergy. *General Directory for Catechesis* (GDC). Washington, D.C.: United States Catholic Conference, 1998.

The GDC includes a general definition of catechesis and its goals and essential elements, along with guidelines for drafting national catechisms and catechetical directories. For use in conjunction with the *Catechism* by bishops, clergy, and diocesan and parish educators.

National Conference of Catholic Bishops

(CHRONOLOGICAL ORDER)

Program of Social Reconstruction. 1919. In *Pastoral Letters of the United States Catholic Bishops*. Vol. 1: 1792–1940. Washington, D.C.: United States Catholic Conference, 1984.

In the wake of World War I, this document of the administrative committee of the National Catholic War Council lays out principles and recommendations for social reconstruction and reform.

Brothers and Sisters to Us. 1979. Washington, D.C.: United States Catholic Conference, 1979.

This is the landmark pastoral letter from the U.S. bishops in which they promote discussion and action against racism, "an evil which endures in our society and in our Church."

The Challenge of Peace: God's Promise and Our Response. 1983. Washington, D.C.: United States Catholic Conference, 1983.

This pastoral letter summarizes the Church's teaching on peacemaking and applies this tradition to the issues of nuclear weapons and the arms race.

Economic Justice for All: Pastoral Letter on Catholic Social Teaching and the U.S. Economy. 1986. Washington, D.C.: United States Catholic Conference, 1987.

This pastoral letter summarizes major principles of Catholic social teaching regarding the economy and addresses morally significant economic issues in the United States.

A Century of Social Teaching: A Common Heritage, a Continuing Challenge. 1990. Washington, D.C.: United States Catholic Conference, 1990.

This brief statement summarizes the basic themes of Catholic social teaching. It was published to mark the hundredth anniversary of *Rerum Novarum.*

Renewing the Earth: An Invitation to Reflection and Action on Environment in Light of Catholic Social Teaching. 1991. Washington, D.C.: United States Catholic Conference, 1992.

This document explores environmental challenges and is the first major treatment of the moral dimensions of the ecological crisis by the U.S. bishops.

Communities of Salt and Light: Reflections on the Social Mission of the Parish. 1993. Washington, D.C.: United States Catholic Conference, 1994.

This document is a resource for strengthening the parish's social mission and infusing social teaching into all aspects of parish life.

The Harvest of Justice Is Sown in Peace: A Reflection of the National Conference of Catholic Bishops on the Tenth Anniversary of "The Challenge of Peace." 1994. Washington, D.C.: United States Catholic Conference, 1994.

This reflection addresses the dangers of U.S. isolationism, the value of nonviolence, the just-war theory, humanitarian intervention, deterrence, conscientious objection, and the development of peoples.

A Decade After "Economic Justice for All": Continuing Principles, Changing Context, New Challenges. 1995. Washington, D.C.: United States Catholic Conference, 1995.

This pastoral message marks the tenth anniversary of *Economic Justice for All* and, using the principles in the original pastoral, explores economic challenges.

Called to Global Solidarity: International Challenges for U.S. Parishes. 1997. Washington, D.C.: United States Catholic Conference, 1997.

In the tradition of *Communities of Salt and Light,* this statement calls on parishes to integrate global solidarity into all aspects of parish life.

Sharing Catholic Social Teaching: Challenges and Directions: Reflections of the U.S. Catholic Bishops. 1998. Washington, D.C.: United States Catholic Conference, 1998.

This statement summarizes major themes of Catholic social teaching and stresses the need to incorporate it into educational and formational programs.

Everyday Christianity: To Hunger and Thirst for Justice. 1998. Washington, D.C.: United States Catholic Conference, 1998.

This explains that the most important way Catholics work for justice and peace is through their choices and actions every day. The publication also contains information on the jubilee and the lay call to justice.

Faithful Citizenship: Civic Responsibility for a New Millennium. 1999. Washington, D.C.: United States Catholic Conference, 1999.

The U.S. bishops celebrate the Jubilee Year 2000 as "a time to bring together the guidance of the Gospel and the opportunities of our democracy to shape a society more respectful of human life and dignity, and more committed to justice and peace." With hope that "the campaigns and elections of the year 2000 become turning points in our democracy," the bishops encourage all to recommit to active citizenship as the new millennium begins. Interwoven throughout the document are the seven themes of Catholic social teaching and moral priorities for public life.

Recommended Video

Bring Down the Walls. Washington, D.C.: United States Catholic Conference, 1991.

Marking the hundredth anniversary of *Rerum Novarum,* this video was inspired by the fall of the Berlin Wall to depict the call to tear down walls of injustice and indifference. The video covers historical developments and social issues, summarizes principles of Catholic social teaching, and concludes with suggestions for action. (12 minutes)

Other Programs and Materials

Departments of the United States Catholic Conference and the National Conference of Catholic Bishops offer programs to help Catholics respond to Catholic social teaching through service and social transformation. Except as noted, each department is located at 3211 Fourth Street, NE, Washington, DC 20017-1194.

PUBLISHING SERVICES, 800-235-8722— Publishes conciliar, papal, and U.S. bishops' statements on social issues, as well as other resources.

CATHOLIC CAMPAIGN FOR HUMAN DEVELOPMENT (CCHD), 202-541-3210— The U.S. bishops' domestic anti-poverty program. Publishes prayer books, videos, study guides, and materials on social teaching, poverty, and justice.

PRO-LIFE ACTIVITIES, 202-541-3070—Produces a manual, posters, flyers, brochures, and two newsletters on issues within the consistent ethic of life.

SOCIAL DEVELOPMENT AND WORLD PEACE (SDWP), 202-541-3195—Produces resources, manuals, and other materials to accompany bishops' statements on justice and peace.

MIGRATION AND REFUGEE SERVICES (MRS), 202-541-3220—Produces information, materials, and videos on how to "welcome the stranger" into our communities.

CATHOLIC RELIEF SERVICES (CRS), 410-625-2220, 209 WEST FAYETTE STREET, BALTIMORE, MD 21201-3443—The U.S. bishops' overseas development agency. Publishes study materials and videos. Sponsors Operation Rice Bowl, a Lenten program of prayer, fasting, and almsgiving.

NOTES